GREEN AGE

Alicia
Suskin
Ostriker

Green
Age

University of Pittsburgh Press

Published by the University of Pittsburgh Press, Pittsburgh, Pa. 15260
Copyright © 1989, Alicia Suskin Ostriker
All Rights reserved
Baker & Taylor International, London
Manufactured in the United States of America

Library of Congress Cataloging-in-Publication Data

Ostriker, Alicia.
   Green age / Alicia Suskin Ostriker.
      p.   cm. — (Pitt poetry series)
   ISBN 0-8229-3624-0. — ISBN 0-8229-5421-4 (pbk.)
   I. Title. II. Series.
PS3565.S84G7   1989
811'.54—dc20   89-32020
                                        CIP

The author and publisher wish to express their grateful acknowledgment to the following publications in which some of these poems first appeared, sometimes with slightly different titles: *Berkeley Poets Cooperative* ("The Armies of Birds" and "Before Dawn"); *Calyx* ("To Love Is"); *Crosscurrents* ("What You've Given Me"); *5 AM* ("A Day of Heavy Fog" and "The Pure Products of America"); *Iowa Review* ("The Death Ghazals"); *Michigan Quarterly Review* ("A Meditation in Seven Days"); *The Missouri Review* ("Hating the World"); *The Nation* ("I'm Tired of Your Lecturing"); *The Ontario Review* ("American Loneliness," "Cat," "Fifty," "George in Hospital," "Wanting to Be in Love as in Sunlight" and "Words for a Wedding"); *Ploughshares* ("The Cambridge Afternoon Was Gray," "Design," and "Hair"); *Prairie Schooner* ("First Love," "Happy Birthday," "To One in Mourning," "What's Your Name," and "What You Want"); *Poetry* ("Helium," "I Can't Speak," "Moth in April," "Stream," "A Young Woman, a Tree"); *Shenandoah* ("Windshield"); *Southern Humanities Review* ("The Bride"); and *The Threepenny Review* ("Watching the Feeder." "Move" originally appeared in *The New Yorker.*

I am grateful to the Guggenheim Foundation, the Djerassi Foundation, the MacDowell Foundation, and Rutgers University for giving me space and time to work on many of these poems.

The publication of this book is supported by grants from the National Endowment for the Arts in Washington, D.C., a Federal agency, and the Pennsylvania Council on the Arts.

for JPO, with love

Contents

I

The force that through the green fuse drives the flower
Drives my green age; that blasts the roots of trees
Is my destroyer.

—Dylan Thomas

Fifty

This is what a fifty-
Year-old woman looks like,
Said the glamorous feminist
Journalist when they asked her
How it felt to look so young.
A good answer.
But she didn't say, and they didn't
Ask her:
Did you expect the thread
Of your rough childhood
To unwind so far
From its beginnings?
Do you perhaps wonder,
When you try to look backward
And the thread seems invisible, as if
It has been snipped, who
In the world you are,
Stranger?
Do you think: *Let's keep this thing*
Rolling, keep on fighting, keep
Up the good work,
And glare down the steel tracks of the mirror
At the approach of the enemy
Who is still miles away
But coming like a commuter train, do you
Hit your typewriter
Every day, harder
And harder, like a recalcitrant
Spoiled child, have you surrendered
The hope of the perfect
Romance, or do you grip that

Fantasy stubbornly, like a kid holding
On to a dead pet
That she knows is dead

And do you make a joke of all of this
And when the clock says *Almost
Quitting time,* do you still answer *Never?*

A Young Woman, A Tree

The life spills over, some days.
She cannot be at rest,
Wishes she could explode

Like that red tree—
The one that bursts into fire
All this week.

Senses her infinite smallness
But can't seize it,
Recognizes the folly of desire,

The folly of withdrawal—
Kicks at the curb, the pavement,
If only she could, at this moment,

When what she's doing is plodding
To the bus stop, to go to school,
Passing that fiery tree—if only she could

Be making love,
Be making poetry,
Be exploding, be speeding through the universe

Like a photon, like a shower
Of yellow blazes—
She believes if she could only overtake

The riding rhythm of things, of her own electrons,
Then she would be at rest—
If she could forget school,

Climb the tree,
Be the tree,
Burn like that.

ii

She doesn't know yet, how could she,
That this same need
Is going to erupt every September

And that in forty years the idea will strike her
From no apparent source, in a laundromat
Between a washer and a dryer,

Like one of those electric bulbs
Lighting up near a character's head in a comic strip—
There in that naked and soiled place

With its detergent machines,
Its speckled fluorescent lights,
Its lint piles broomed into corners,

As she fumbles for quarters
And dimes, she will start to chuckle and double over
Into the plastic basket's

Mountain of wet
Bedsheets and bulky overalls—
Old lady! She'll grin, beguiled at herself,

Old lady! The desire
To burn is already a burning!
How about that!

iii

Meanwhile the maple
Has also survived, and thinks
It owes its longevity

To its location
Between a bus stop
And a bar, and to its uniquely

Mutant appetite for pollutants:
Carbon monoxide, alcohol, spit . . .
The truth is, it enjoys city life.

Regular working people suffer so grossly
It makes a tree feel happier,
Having nothing to do

But feel its thousand orgasms each spring,
Or stretch its limbs during the windy days
That are like a Swedish massage,

Or swoon into the fall
Among its delicious rain patters,
Its saffron and scarlet flamings.

Then, when the tethered leaves
Snatch themselves away like desperate
Children ardent for freedom,

It will let itself sigh, feel wise
And resigned, and draw
Its thoughts downward to its other crown,

The secret leafless system
That digs in dark
Its thick intelligent arms

And stubborn hands
Under the shops, the streets,
The subways, the granite,

The sewage pipes'
Cold slime,
As deep as that.

Wanting to Be in Love as in Sunlight

I want it even when nobody's loving me
Back, and you say
How regressive, what is the point of that,

Silly woman, etcetera, but listen—
I don't give the orders here,
I follow instructions, I'm often

Confused myself, as if really I ought
To hunker down like a person in a sandstorm
Who all things considered will be lucky

To escape with abrasions, or a blind
Beggar at her station, hearing
The screams go by like crepe paper streamers,

Sirens and stamping feet
That mean a riot's started, and who wouldn't
Feel frightened and helpless then. The loneliness,

Yes, is like walking across the bottom
Of a freezing river, I mean the river
Jordan, the death flow, cold as that. But sometimes

It's this way: your tinny car stops at the top
Of the ferris wheel you're on, so you can rock it
And look down at the fairground

All full of festive people, every color,
Doing their milling around, buying and selling,
Eating their junkfood, the grownups putting away

The Miller Lites, while the little children run
Sucking their Cokes, with a heat that encourages
Gambling at the Po-Ke-No,

Then outside that, a circle of countryside
Like some kind of magic upholstery
For you to rest your eyes on—

It's a scene that's crazy and peaceful together
And hugging your honey, you probably wouldn't mind
Staying right up there.

Helium

—for JPO

For some reason you got up that morning
And decided your balloon was finally
Beginning to give up the ghost
Although, silver and blue, with its friendly caption,
"Happy Birthday," it had been hovering
Up at the ceiling for a month
Like a mild visitor from another planet.
Today you said, "Look, it's inches below the ceiling,"
And there were puckers in it like human skin,
Like the skin of old people.
I knew you were thinking of George, my mother's husband,
A third of a century older than us,
Forgetting to zip his fly, forgetting to wash
Or shave or wipe himself,
Saying and saying it to you: "Jerry, don't get old,"
Man to man, in a voice like someone banging
On a hollow pipe.
You were thinking about his bristly gray cheeks,
His desperate eyes, his advanced obsession with food,
So you cut the balloon's tether,
Pulled on a pair of pants
And we both went outside, still in bare feet,
To stand in the street and watch you release it.
It rose up slowly,
Missed the maples in our front yard, was caught
In a current of breeze and rose faster,
Was becoming distant from us,
Then darted behind a neighbor's copper beech
On the next block and we lost it.
After waiting awhile we took the *New York Times*
From the driveway and went on in for breakfast.
It was still springtime, the sun already high,
And your balloon was either still ascending
Or stopped in the arms of a tree. We couldn't know which,
And we were glad of this.

11

George in Hospital

For a while, in the hospital,
He could sit in his wheelchair, with his diapers tucked
Under green cotton gown,
And watch the people walking past his room.
It was lively and interesting. The nurses
Were pretty and brisk. The doctors were tall
And confident as princes. "Oh," he could say,
"These doctors are really tall. They're a tall bunch."
He could mislay my name, but ask
After my kids, faking it, saying
"Oh yeah, what sweethearts." He could ask:
"Can I please lie down in my bed now?"
He could raise his leathery yellowed feet:
"Can't somebody cut my toenails, please?
Oh, it's terrible." He could still
Push out a voice like traprock down a chute,
The hunks of gravel grating against metal,
To yell, "Oh Mary and Jesus,
This is terrible."

Jersey Transit

—for E. B. White: "City which not to look upon would be like death"

i

That black woman with the extraordinary earrings
Haranguing that black man about the contradictions
Of society, challenging his world-view, she's
Been doing it since the icy Trenton platform
Where the rest of us shivered and looked at our watches.
Doctrinally correct, but
He's tired from work and
He's just been helplessly viewing her breasts
The whole trip between Trenton and New Brunswick.

ii

Father and son in the aisle, the man's
Mouth is hair-thin; nose too; it would seem he exercises
Much control. He is pointing something out
Among the grimy smokestacks of Elizabeth—
Telephone wires? A church? His boy looks aside and says:
"Forget it, dad."

iii

The elderly passenger, the young conductor, negotiate.
The old man puts his
Change in his pocket, leans back
Against the seat and picks his teeth.
The train rattles along, making us all
Fall half-asleep.
Over the dank Jersey horizon the World Trade Center rises
Like a pair of angels
Or a pair of gigantic tusks
And soon the train will dive into the tunnel, emerging
As if newborn, into the mammoth
Starlit City. The young conductor
Comes back again and touches the man's shoulder.

Moth in April

Can I concentrate, can I
Let my eyes and mind settle
On the papery bug

That has settled on the wood
Knob of the canvas
Garden chair

In my friend's backyard, that is
So early humming with bees, and is
Supposed to be relaxing—

The moth has to be thinking.
Its moth-face frowns.
The hair feelers, black-tipped, stand level.

It jumps and flies and I have
No words to describe its pin-jag track.
It flies away from the knob and back,

My fuzzy likeness,
My brother, seizing me with melancholy—
I'm on edge, it could be the coffee

And not enough sleep,
Could be the sense of all I cannot see
And cannot feel, and will die without learning.

A Birthday Suite

—for Eve

1. The Cambridge Afternoon Was Gray

When you were born, the nurse's aide
Wore a gray uniform, and the Evelyn Nursing Home
Was full of Sisters of Mercy starched

To a religious ecstasy
Of tidiness. They brought you, struggling feebly
Inside your cotton blanket, only your eyes

Were looking as if you already knew
What thinking would be like—
Some pinch of thought was making your eyes brim

With diabolic relish, like a child
Who has been hiding crouched down in a closet
Among the woolen overcoats and stacked

Shoeboxes, while the anxious parents
Call *Where are you?* And suddenly the child
Bounces into the room

Pretending innocence. . . . My hot breast
Was delighted, and ran up to you like a dog
To a younger dog it wants to make friends with,

So the scandalized aide had to pull the gray
Curtains around our bed, making a sound
Of hissing virtue, curtainrings on rod,

While your eyes were saying *Where am I? I'm here!*

2. *Bitterness*

Somebody said of you when you were young,
"That child hates being a child"
—It explained or seemed to explain your resistance

To love, the creamy family food
I tried to dish out. So against my will
I had to look at you, the little daughter,

Where you sat glumly on bare linoleum
Hitting a block with another block,
Until I felt it, the humiliation

Of childhood helplessness, the ugliness
Of the giant omnivores who
Never listened, never understood,

Who always kept on shoving you around
For your own good. You looked
Settled as if you knew you were

The final piece of fruit
Left in a festive bowl while the noisy guests
Go right ahead with their toasting and spilling,

A solitary apple, unripe, stunted,
But keeping busy catalyzing the bitterness
Under its peel: an apple nobody wanted

Or was ever going to want.

3. *Cat*

If a cat can be ugly, Tiger was ugly.
A nothing color, the color of ash.
A coward, flinching

From anyone's shoes,
The desperate thin mind of a terrorist
As if we had plucked him from Belfast, biting

And clawing the hand that fed
Or attempted caress, drawing blood, inscribing
I will avenge in the long scratch marks

The wicked pee, the pitiable
Attacks of vomiting,
And you

Loved him, you alone loved him
The way we have to love the world, have to
Keep on loving it, like passing some kind of test

That God seems to be setting us. His bowls
Of Kitty Chow and water laid
By a clean litterbox, his fur petted,

You would pucker your brow, *good Tiger, good Tiger,*
Lifting him from the German prison camps
From the South American torturers to your lap

Smelling of young girl, making him see reason.

4. Design

Curled on the sofa she does her problem sets.
Her auburn hair cascades, her fingers write,
Her sighs heave, according to a formula

For which we'll never learn the equations.
Okay, what makes this phototropic tendril
Lift itself into air, place itself outward

So, upward so? Some code is being
Decoded in some control room, essential decisions
Are occurring every moment. The parents pretend

To go about their business, while casting
Furtive glances at the plant in their midst.
They have appeared to drive to work, come home,

Eat dinner and dessert. Actually,
They are holding onto the arboretum railing,
While the stalks emerge, fork,

Burst into leaves! Now they have almost forgotten
The way for years it was darkish prickles,
Tightest of wrappings, until

The thorn-leaves fell, and she stepped out like a girl
In a fairy tale, all stingless, all petals,
All infinite bits of pollen—

The elegant proof, the argument from design.

5. *Hair*

When I was the privileged woman I wiped
The hair from your forehead
With its childish pucker, moist as a washcloth

And when I was queen I brushed and braided it
Pulled it away from your ears at the breakfast table
Your ears as complicated as carnations—

Thus year followed year, like the eyeblink that human time
Really is, until you decided
I did it poorly, you could do it better, tighter

Yourself. So you brushed me off
But my nose could reconstruct your ripe scalp-smell,
My palms the raw-silk feel of your springy strands.

When finally you sat in the hairdresser chair,
Child hair chopped off, as loose as brush
Around a clearing where someone is going to build,

I adored your face that rose, abrupt and pure,
A moon rising to survey the planet
By its own lucidity, while my hands

Were like lucky exiles who get away with everything.
Years after the revolution they still recall
The velvet ropes at the opera, that feel

Of utter unmistakable luxury.

6. First Love

When the child begins to suffer, the mother
Finds in her mouth those burning coals
You can neither spit out nor swallow—

It tells you about this in Zen, you know
You're illuminated when
The coals dissolve and your mouth is cool—

The child's lost boyfriend permeates the home
Like hyacinth perfume,
Nothing can escape it, it is too much,

It is maddening, like the insane yellow
Of the first blooming forsythia, like a missing
Limb that goes on hurting the survivor.

Whatever doesn't suffer isn't alive,
You know your daughter's pain is perfectly normal.
Nevertheless you imagine

Rinsing all grief from the child's tender face
The way a sculptor might peel the damp dropcloths
Off the clay figure she's been working on

So she can add fresh clay, play
With some details, pat it, bring it closer
To completion, and so people can see

How good and beautiful it already is.

7. Happy Birthday

Happy birthday, a gray day like the first one—
You were so brave to enter our world
With its dirty rain, its look of a sepia photograph.

I call you at college, early and drowsy.
I hear you describe the party last night,
How you danced, how dancing is one of the things

You love in your life, like thinking hard. You are
All right, then, and on the telephone
Hearing the high snaredrum of your voice

I can feel you about to be born, I can feel
The barriers yield as you slide
Along the corrugated glitter,

Like some terrible rubbery ocean built of blood
That parts at a touch, leaving a path.
"What should I do," you wonder, "after I graduate?"

Now I imagine you curled under your quilt
As a cold light begins to enter
Like a knife in a pirate's teeth. Dear salt flesh,

I am ready if you are, I am afraid if you are.
I still ask: will this hurt, will it give pleasure,
Will I survive it? On your mark, get set,

We give birth to each other. Welcome. Welcome.

Before Dawn

The hour before dawn, there is
My young courageous cousin
Orion, setting again,
And myself wakened from my dream.
Only in the dream am I
Powerful and great enough to push
The ocean liner down the
Strand, through the pebbles, almost
Soundlessly, a hush, a shush
Until its prow finally
Touches tide and its entire
Form slides calmly
Away, like a grown child,
Or a book packed with language,
Or a penis slipping quietly
Into a woman.
Only in the dream can I hear
Seawater rushing ashore
While the ship diminishes
And phosphorus lights the foam.

The Secret Sharer

How many times in childhood, you were running
And fell, and ripped your knees on the sidewalk—
Wasn't there something fascinating
About that transformation, the oozing out
Of your crimson blood from the torn plush
Cushion of skin all streaked and swollen
That hideous mix of yellow, violet, and dirt?
Something to gaze at, something to exhibit,
Where a minute ago was nothing,
Somebody having to pick the gravel pieces
Out of your bloody flesh.

So much childhood pain, a girl who hit you,
A boy spitting in your face,
A teacher's laughter at you,
Your mother's grief, like drilling through steel,
And then in winter you were always cold,
The mean wind cutting through your flimsy coat.

Wasn't there always a pair of eyes
Quite calmly looking at things through your eyes
Like a tourist admiring the panorama?
Wasn't there that microphone, where brainstem
Intersects cerebellum, instructing you
In a delicate musical voice
To pay attention to all you saw?

A child stiffened by glory or fear,
Sometimes flying right through the ceiling of sorrow,
As if it were merely paper,
Into a room that was somehow larger—
Did you ever think to ask *Who's there?*
No, and you still don't know.

Watching the Feeder

Snow has been falling, and the purple finches
Attack the feeder, diving like air aces.
A half a dozen squirrels
Do their Olympic leaps through the weak sunlight
Spilling sunflower seeds and seedhusks
Together over the drifts. The doves are pacing
And nodding, with the utmost
Placidity, like bourgeois wives and husbands.
Apparently they are going shopping—
I can almost see the stoutness of their billfolds,
Their station wagons, their wine cellars.
Snow falls through standing trees, my patch of the world's hair.

I have Vivaldi on the stereo,
Another cup of coffee. It is peaceful but hard
Growing older, no
Birds in my nest.

Now I can ask: What about my life?
What do I desire, now
That it has come to this? Snow coming down
Harder and harder this morning, the back yard
Becomes mysterious, the feeder
Is finally deserted.
I remember that I was hoping to be grateful
For existence itself.

American Loneliness

American loneliness joins us, it is the truth,
You with your bottle, your head falling,
You with your wallet
And polished shoes, no better off.
You feeling the basketball lift
Like the mercy of Christ from your fingers, and you
Hitting that meager child.
You over there, jeering—I'm talking to you.

We keep on meeting, like clandestine lovers
Under a rainy October lamp-post,
In a forties movie with the war still on.
Or look at us—I know you're not feeling well—
Coiled in the fuming back seat of a Greyhound
Speeding between two cities, an April twilight,
Through American loneliness, which is the worst.

The buds are out, out in the chill.
The sky goes yellow, yellow-green,
Neon comes on in the dumpy towns
And at the turnpike exits.
You've had a fever, plase try to sleep.

Or maybe we are in the Edward Hopper
Where the night is closing down just past
The all-night gas station, swallowing the road
And the bushes. Maybe we're in a shack
Somewhere behind those bushes, and we're tired
Of no work and no money
And we're listening to crickets shriek
With that harshness of theirs that is almost consoling.

II

I will rise now, and go about the city in the streets,
and in the broad ways I will seek him whom my soul
loveth: I sought him but I found him not.

The watchmen that go about the city found me: to whom I
said, Saw ye him whom my soul loveth?

—The Song of Solomon

Stream

With swift delusional energy:
That's how my best student in '67
Described a rushing

Stream, and I have forgotten
Neither the phrase nor his series
Of quick disintegrations over the next

Few years, a river dropping
Down a flight of steps. It wasn't the acid
He dropped in Vietnam did this, it was the people

He dropped,
That is to say he killed,
He and his army buddies, and took

Personally, I knew because his hands shook
If he tried to talk
About it, and then he'd stop

Out of deference to me perhaps:
Young, I had never seen a person's hands
Shaking. Maybe he'd tell

A bitter joke on the nuns
Who raised him in South Jersey,
Mocking their gestures, and then clutch

His body, small and strong
Like my husband's. I recall his tidy mustache,
The braying giggle that confused the other students

Before he dropped out. I recall there is
A difference between illusion
And delusion, the *maya*

That sustains us, flimsy ghosts in a flimsy world,
And the madness
And suffering that destroy us. The stream isn't

Delusional, I say, it represents
A truth, the actual motion of all matter,
All energy in its interior

Secret torrent that's invisible
To my stupid human
Eye, and it is also

The image of those minds
That smash one way, downhill,
Downhill, amid the spray

Of their uncontrollable
Meditations, downhill,
Slowly or swiftly

Without peace, without hope,
Letting themselves be broken, time
After time, by stone

After stone, and I believe the raging,
The flying water is real,
The tons of it, only

I hate the frozen snowfields
It descends from, a delusional
Purity, and the brutal

Rock that rends it,
A delusional
Solidity.

Hating the World

I hate the world! you scream
At me over the telephone.
I translate fast, it means
That you hate me.
Somehow it's my fault
That you are unhappy, that your job
At the scummy motel demeans you
And you won't quit, that you don't have a lover
Or work to do that you love.

You're getting old, almost forty,
You who were once my student,
Almost my lover, only
You like men better, or fear them less.
What was it, our friendship?
A little sexual aura, a little faith
In spiritual truth, some book chat
And some wild, stoned joking?

You used to wear sweaters with holes
At the elbows and carry your lunch
Of fruits in a brown paper bag.
You liked the flaky edge of rock and roll.
Once you announced, ethereal,
You'd learned in the midnight park
How the entire earth was a sort of dancing,
Even the maple leaves the size of your palm,
Even the Chevrolets speeding past on the highway.

Do you know, to hate the world
Makes you my enemy?
I love the world, I reply
Sticking the knife in.
I'm trying to help, I mutter
Twisting it.

The Pure Products of America

In the middle of the Southeast Asian war
When my poetry students would drive
Down from New Brunswick
To meet in my apartment,
See my family, sit on floor, drink wine—
This one sometimes might
Appear, dressed in his
Bob Dylan outfit, black
Scuffy boots, bluejeans, torn
Flannel shirt, black
Leather motorcycle jacket
And a black hat with a brim
To hide his timid face under.
He didn't talk. Late
In the evening he might extract
From his jeans pocket a many-folded
Piece of paper, and
Read the poem on it, a carnival
Or a barnyard, blowing us
Away. He wasn't actually
In the class, but nobody cared about
Things like that then, and Luke was good in ways
We liked, he despised the war, demanded sex
And love for all, in America's own
Vulgarly exhilarating speech
That cats and dogs can figure out,
Tamping it down with dynamite imagery,
Like Rimbaud, and with cadences
Out of rhythm and blues. We all knew
Boys like that. What happened
To this one, he went west
And somehow wrong, America the Beautiful
Too ugly or too toxic. Underwent
Some jail, some hospital, the medication,
The things the experts did then, when a person
Without a lot of money slid

Into the funny Asian jungle
That's right at home, to ensure
They would never return
With information for us. Luke still writes
Me letters, it's about twenty years,
Pages half legible in a childish hand.
He thinks he's a detective, only
They put poison in my head
Is what he says, *It*
Slows me down, baby, the therapy—
I used to write him back
But I wish he'd quit.

Windshield

You are supposed to roll your windows up
Driving through certain neighborhoods
Because they are waiting for you at the intersections,
For you or anyone,
Where cars go bumper to bumper,
Flirtatious shadows, wanting to clean your windshield,
Perhaps, or to shoot you, the way they shot my friend
The talkative flutist, lost on Detroit's avenues,
Through his open old Ford window.
Got him in the cheek and shoulder,
No reason. He was just busy talking, and the summer
Evening was stifling.
Up at the red light now, they are doing their crisp dance
With their rags and squeegees
Around a helpless Subaru.
Watch it, mister—
A warrior strut, a cottonmouth snap to remind you
Of the wet odor of rural underbrush,
A little twirl, a little
Hustle on oily cobblestones.
When one of them advances on you, yellow eyes
And shining teeth, denim slung
Low on a wasted pelvis, you can feel
In your bones the awful
Cruelty of his life,
As looking at you sitting behind windowglass
Just at the moment you resist the urge
Your foot has, to jam on the gas,
He sees that blank expression flattening
Your face like a heavy drug, and he
Can feel the cruelty
Of yours, man, right in his bones.

The Death Ghazals

If a raindrop enters the ocean, good.
It is where it yearned to be.

If it enters the soil, good.
Let's hope something will grow.

They thought like this for thousands of years
While the clean dead refreshed the ground.

Heroes lay with the ash-spears through their brains
And Homer sang of them, striking the harp.

Stomachs of girls forgot the hours of childbirth
Under the lawns, in the swept tombs.

The skin of the deeply old, among stones,
Kept helping the lovers to kiss.

Today even the rainstorms are poisoned—
Bleak dust, a sterilized lake, infected forests—

Ghostly buffalo stand in your car's headlights
And you drive right through them.

ii

Something exciting is kicking through the sperm,
The capillaries, the plasma, and now it's home.

They love this house! They've dusted and polished, they've
    brought
Their own expensive silver.

The committeemen loosen their neckties, there ought to be
A law, or so they claim. They arrange their papers.

Hath the rain a father? Shall we seal the border?
Nature is a law also, like *need*, like *night*.

Like a needle, the word *death*
Is easily mislaid. The word *pestilential*.

Ripe bloodspots, there and there, on the moon's face,
Make her a swollen whore, and no more maiden.

Three-deep along the leather bar, a jacket, a hip, a saxophone
Wails and rotates on its gummy axle.

For sticks and rags, try looking at a puppet
When the master removes his hand.

iii

—D. K., *1932–1986*

Now your old teacher and friend
Is traveling the highway backward.

Straight as a yardstick, it runs toward a canal
Where a boat bumps gently against logs.

Billboards wing past, offering salutations,
Two crows alight on a telephone wire.

Palaces, churches, a glorious morning
Ripens toward noon, even in narrow alleyways.

He is trying to hold his head high
As the water smell approaches.

He is pink
And hairless, like a newborn mouse.

Are you ready to pray yet? Are you ready to light candles?
Closer. Come on closer. Are you ready to go to the concert?

—for Suzanne Vega

Whatever doesn't suffer isn't alive.
Student number one, will you kindly comment?

Increased consciousness: potential for charm and sanity,
For acute pain, for self and others. Your choice.

A holier healing, a more efficient torture—
Remind me if this is the dance of Shiva.

I'm trying to remember something. Wasn't it illumination,
The crests of sex?

Girl of ice at the party, you stand at the bathroom sink,
Throwing up your bitterness, along with your last drink.

Papa, you gave her a silk dress from Saigon,
Saying, "Don't ask me where I got it from."

"The exalted mirror can go to hell," laugh the courtesans
Of Greece, and Italy, and imperial China.

Where there's life there's hope. We bequeath this hope
To our children, along with our warm tears.

And I won't even mention the crying of orphans
that reaches up to the throne of God and
beyond, making
a circle with no end and no god.
—Yehudah Amichai

Not having found you in music or mathematics
They look for you, my God, on the battlefield.

Blind fiery hope propels them,
A Promethean gift, an illusion.

"You can't see anything through the fire
But the fire itself, and it's so smoky."

"And the intense heat when you approach
Hurls you backward, but it's so marvelous."

Bodies of brothers are dropping like soot.
High in the air, gunfire rattle and cannon hoot.

Ecstasy of pain, drawn across the dirt
Into which it is coughing blood, to the Red Cross station—

Clad in ironic olive, on both sides
Boys fight, who have scarcely learned to shave—

At last they feel alive! They have discovered
What they were made for, from the very cradle.

Amid carnage they are altogether joyous
For they believe they see you striding there.

Is it true, is it true, are you a champion?
Does your smeared forehead out-top the gracious mountains?

You Who Deny: A Harangue

I would like to bury
all the hating eyes.
—Anne Sexton

You who deny, my impulse is to shake you
As an abusive mother shakes her child:
Its loose skin like a kitten's, and her own voice
An emergency, a siren wail
Lifting off like the streak from the Münch painting,
She throws her child at the wall because resisting
This passion is too difficult, she slaps
The wet cheek: *Now you will finally stop*
Being silly and stubborn, will listen, believe,
Obey. A lie, she knows that, and cannot wipe
Knowledge away with hitting and screaming. Some falsity
Props up all wickedness, even when we know it:
The addict knows *I need this, I need it*
Is a lie, the killer knows *It doesn't matter*
If someone dies is a lie

Yet they go on and on.

> You who deny,
I have watched you squat over the frightened children
While you squeeze welfare money from their mothers
To feed another aircraft carrier,
I have watched your hardhats build Key West villas
For the wealthy and jailcells for the poor,
I have seen your flag rippling in the breeze
Over burned villages, over Swiss banks,
Over Bangkok brothels, where it sings O Beautiful
For Spacious Skies,
I have seen your lawyers step, dainty as weevils,
Over the sad farmhouse,
I have interviewed your receptionist explaining
She didn't invent the rules, and I have monitored
Your midnight flight across the Bolivian border,

40

Each spit-white brick in your hold
As thrilling as murder.

The printout in my hand stares at me mockingly.
It already knows my merely human arguments.
When I beg it to debate, it declines,
When I reach for its mask
It slides rings on its fingers,
When I show it my daughter's
Dazzling smile, it is busy signing paychecks,
When I offer my son's sweet tenor, and my mother's
Contralto laughter, it makes choking noises,
When I lend it my husband's brainful of stars
It reels from the machine sticking its tongue out.

Now it is climbing into its stretch limousine,
It is sorry it has no time. When I seize its shoulders
Like a crab, to cry *Oh please, oh please,*
Aren't you mortal like me, and don't you need
Something to love, it telephones the police,
It lights a cigar, it raises its eyebrows, it dares me
To strike it

        And I want to, in fact I want to
Kill it. O you who deny,
To surrender to your malignity is fatal,
To struggle against your infection is fatal,
Yet we go on, not knowing why, like someone
Climbing the hill of illness, that hard breast,
That stone blister, that moonlit desert slope
Of martyred cactus, that mother without compassion,
Taking it step by step, one
Breath at a time
We go on.

A Day of Heavy Fog

A day of heavy fog
Swirls up from the Pacific, a day of wind—

Blue gray and olive gray, the giant redwoods
Lining the canyon stand sighing in their ranks,

A shallow webbing of roots holding all of them up,
Pulling this moisture in through their million glossy

Bottle green needles, like the veterans
Of a decimated regiment

Growing slowly drunk on a warm Saturday evening—
Escaped from their sorrowing daughters, their baritone voices

Ascend: stiff as a crutch, maintaining their dignity
They make song out of suffering,

They will sing fights and murders, they will sing noble
Battles lost, young fellows lost,

They will damn in melodious rant
The pig generals, the officers, the informers,

They will curse the enemy,
The civilians, the food,

The land itself, by Christ, and if little enough
Remains save drunkenness and song,

The more's the need of staying absolutely upright
No matter what else happens.

The Bride

i

Jerusalem sits on her mountains, a woman
Who knits and frowns, going over and over her story,
Sifting it, every detail memorized, magnified,
Interpreted. How many lovers, what caresses, what golden
Fornications, what children of brilliant intellect
Sucking hard at her nipples,
What warriors, what artists.

There was a time for riches, a time for poverty.
She has gone begging in the streets, yes,
And she has danced in her rags.

And today they are killing for her
Among the stones. What woman would not
Be thoroughly proud. They love her, they love her
Above the queens
Of the earth, above the other beauties.

ii

The cats in Jerusalem form the secret
Government. They are sisters. They have hearts
As black as eels, or hearts as red
And wise as pomegranates.

They insinuate everywhere, everywhere.
Under the shady orange trees
Sit three or four,
By the ruined wall a score,
Nine surround the Dome of the Rock.
Six yawn, their mouths open as orchids,
Revealing needle teeth.

So forget the rabbis and their frozen Law,
A rod that likes

Hitting a child's fingers, and making
That satisfying sting of punishment.
Forget about the members
Of Parliament, shouting yet reasonable
Like jewelry merchants counting on your goodwill.
Forget the competitive brands of Christians
Selling postcards of sexy crucifixions
Who peer from shadowy galleries of the Church
Of the Holy Sepulchre, its livid saints
And martyrs dissolving into grimy mosaic darkness.
Forget the revolutionary students.
Cheap thrills, cheap thrills.
Forget even the fleshy mothers
Sarah and Hagar,
Praying, shopping, cooking,
Complaining. Forget their apartments, their leaky
Sinks, and the shortened screams when the bad news comes
On the evening radio about their sons
Who were tall and handsome, who were slightly careless
In Hebron, or the Golan, or Beirut.

Forget the mayor, his rosy stitching and patching.
Forget making the world a better place.

Blood and sand.
What is reality and what is fiction?
The cats crouch, the cats
Have a saying: You've seen one corpse,

You've seen them all. The black, the white, the gray,
Stealthy, overt, and sleek,
The runners, the striped ones,
The ones that look like apricots and milk,
Are receiving orders from a small, blackened
Bronze Egyptian cat
In the Rockefeller Museum
Near the Damascus gate,
The cat of dire memory, whose heart,
The size of an olive, is heavier
Than an iron cannonball.

Heavy because so angry,
So angry.

A Meditation in Seven Days

i

> *Hear O Israel*
> *the Lord our God*
> *the Lord is One*
> —Deuteronomy 6:4

If your mother is a Jew, you are a Jew
—Here is the unpredictable

Residue, but of what archaic power
Why the chain of this nation matrilineal

When the Holy One, the One
Who creates heaven and earth from formless void

Is utterly, violently masculine, with his chosen
Fathers and judges, his kings

And priests in their ritual linen, their gold and blue,
And purple and scarlet, his prophets clothed only

In a ragged vision of righteousness, angry
Voices promising a destructive fire

And even in exile, his rabbis with their flaming eyes
The small boys sent to the house of study

To sit on the benches
To recite, with their soft lips, a sacred language

To become the vessels of memory,
Of learning, of prayer,

Across the vast lands of the earth, kissing
His Book, though martyred, though twisted

Into starving rags, in
The village mud, or in wealth and grandeur

Kissing his Book, and the words of the Lord
Became fire on their lips

—What were they all but men in the image
Of God, where is their mother

❋

The lines of another story, inscribed
And reinscribed like an endless chain

A proud old woman, her face desert-bitten
Has named her son: laughter

Laughter for bodily pleasure, laughter for old age triumph
Hagar the rival stumbles away

In the hot sand, along with her son Ishmael
They nearly die of thirst, God pities them

But among us each son and daughter
Is the child of Sarah, whom God made to laugh

❋

Sarah, legitimate wife
Woman of power

My mother is a Jew, I am a Jew
Does it teach me enough

In the taste of every truth a sweeter truth
In the bowels of every injustice an older injustice

In memory
A tangle of sandy footprints

47

ii

Whoever teaches his daughter Torah,
teaches her obscenity.
—Rabbi Eleazer

If a woman is a Jew
Of what is she the vessel

If she is unclean in her sex, if she is
Created to be a defilement and a temptation

A snake with breasts like a female
A succubus, a flying vagina

So that the singing of God
The secret of God

The name winged in the hues of the rainbow
Is withheld from her, so that she is the unschooled

Property of her father, then of her husband
And if no man beside her husband

May lawfully touch her hand
Or gaze at her almond eyes, if when the dancers

Ecstatically dance, it is not with her,
Of what is she the vessel

If a curtain divides her prayer
From a man's prayer—

We shall burn incense to the queen of heaven, and shall pour her liba-
tions as we used to do, we, our fathers, our kings and our princes, in the
cities of Judah and in the streets of Jerusalem. For then we had plenty
of food and we were all well and saw no evil. —Jeremiah 44:17

Solomon's foreign wives, and the Canaanite daughters
Who with Ishtar mourned the death of Tammuz

Who *on the high places, under every green tree, and alongside*
The altars set fig boughs, images of Ashtoreth

Who *offered incense to the queen of heaven*
And sang in a corner of the temple, passing from hand to hand

In token of joy the fruited branch, body
Of the goddess their mothers loved

Who made cakes bearing her features
And their husbands knew

The Lady of Snakes
The Lady of Lilies

She who makes prosper the house
Who promulgates goodness, without whom is famine

Cursed by the furious prophet, scattered screaming
Burned alive according to law, for witchcraft

Stoned to death by her brothers, perhaps by men
She has nakedly loved, for the free act of love

In her city square
Her eyes finally downcast

Her head shaved
Is she too the vessel of memory

For out of Zion shall go forth the law, and the word of the Lord from Jerusalem. And he shall judge among the nations, and shall rebuke many people: and they shall beat their swords into plowshares, and their spears into pruninghooks: nation shall not lift up sword against nation, neither shall they learn war any more.   —Isaiah 2:3-4

Here is another story: the ark burned,
The marble pillars buried, the remnant scattered

A thousand years, two thousand years
In every patch of the globe, the gentle remnant

Of whom our rabbis boast: *Compassionate sons
Of compassionate fathers*

In love not with the Law, but with the kindness
They claim to be the whole of the Torah

Torn from a whole cloth
From the hills of Judea

That ran with sweetness, and from the streams
That were jewels, yearning for wholeness, next

Year in Jerusalem, surely, there would be
Milk and honey, they could see

The thing plainly, an ideal society
Of workers, the wise, the holy hill flowing

Finally with righteousness—
Here they are, in the photographs of the 1880s,

The young women, with their serious eyes
Their lace collars and cameo brooches

Are the partners of these serious young men
Who stand shaven, who have combed their hair smoothly

They are writing pamphlets together, which describe
In many little stitches the word *shalom*

They have climbed out of the gloomy villages
They have kissed the rigid parents good-bye

Soon they will be a light to the nations
They will make the desert bloom, they are going to form

The plough and pruninghook Isaiah promised
After tears of fire, of blood, of mud

Of the sword and shame
Eighty generations

Here in their eyes the light of justice from Sinai
And the light of pure reason from Europe

I intend to convict God for murder, for he is destroying his people and the Law he gave them from Mount Sinai. I have irrefutable proof in my hands. —Elie Wiesel, *The Gates of the Forest*

And Esau said unto his father, Hast thou but one blessing, my father? Bless me, even me also, O my father. And Esau lifted up his voice, and wept. —Genesis 27:38

Does the unanswered prayer
Corrode the tissue of heaven

Doesn't it rust the wings
Of the heavenly host, shouldn't it

Untune their music, doesn't it become
Acid splashed in the face of the king

Smoke, and the charred bone bits suspended in it
Sifting inevitably upward

Spoiling paradise
Spoiling even the dream of paradise

vi

Come, my friend, come, my friend
Let us go to meet the bride
—Sabbath Song

And in between she would work and clean and cook. But the food, the food: salmon croquettes, clam cakes, casseroles, cream puffs, sweet and sour meatballs, and then, through the years, as you and your sister left and money was looser, escalating in gourmet finesse, spinach crepes, sole amandine, soufflés and vichyssoise and chiffon pie. O the visits were filled with food. —Melanie Kaye/Kantrowitz

Not speculation, nothing remote
No words addressed to an atomic father

Not the wisdom of the wise
Nor a promise, and not the trap of hereafter

Here, now, through the misted kitchen windows
Since dawn the dusk is falling

Everywhere in the neighborhood
Women have rushed to the butcher, the grocer

With a violet sky she prepares the bread, she plucks
And cooks the chicken, grates the stinging horseradish

These are her fingers, her sinewy back as she scrubs
The house, her hands slap the children and clean them

Dusk approaches, wind moans
Food ready, it is around her hands

The family faces gather, the homeless
She has gathered like sheep, it is her veiny hands

That light the candles, so that suddenly
Our human grief illuminated, we're a circle

53

Practical and magical, it's
Strong wine and food time coming, and from outside time

From the jewelled throne
Of a house behind history

She beckons the bride, the radiant
Sabbath, the lady we share with God

Our mother's palms like branches lifted in prayer
Lead our rejoicing voices, our small chorus

Our clapping hands in the here and now
In a world that is never over

And never enough

vii

For lo, the winter is past; the rain is over and gone; The flowers appear on the earth; the time of the singing of birds is come.
—Song of Solomon 2:11-12

What can I possess
But the history that possesses me

With whom I must wrestle
But myself

And as to the father, what is his trouble
That leaves him so exhausted and powerless

Why is he asleep, his gigantic
Limbs pulseless, dispersed over the sky

White, unnerved
No more roar

He who yesterday threatened murder, yanking
At his old uniform, waving his dress sword

He's broken every glass in the house, the drunkard
He's snapped the sticks of furniture, howling

And crying, liquor spilled everywhere
He's staggered to the floor, and lies there

In filth, three timid children prod him
While screwing their faces up from the stink

That emanates from his mouth—
He has beaten them black and blue

But they still love him, for
What other father have they, what other king—

He begins to snore, he is dreaming again
How outside the door a barefoot woman is knocking

Snakes slide downhill in the forest
Preparing to peel themselves in rebirth, wriggling

Fiddlehead ferns uncurl, a square of blue sky
Flings its veil, pale mushrooms

Raise their noses after the downpour
A breeze rustles through her yellow dress

Don't come back, he whispers in his sleep
Like a man who endures a nightmare

And in my sleep, in my twentieth century bed
It's that whisper I hear, *go away,*

Don't touch, so that I ask
Of what am I the vessel

Fearful, I see my hand is on the latch
I am the woman, and about to enter

III

And soon I will know I was talking to my own soul.
—Adrienne Rich

Homage to Rumi: Seven Poems

1. The Armies of Birds

While we were asleep, the armies
Of birds arrived, and are filling the world with song.
That flat, miserable brownness
We remember has vanished.
The first blue crocuses struggle
From under the earth and kneel
In the sunlight. Get up,
Get dressed, friend!
The police are throwing their caps
And badges away.

Whoever stays sober in this weather
Is afraid of what the neighbors will say.

2. I Can't Speak

God is the Being . . . that may
properly only be addressed, not expressed.
—Martin Buber, *I and Thou*

It's hopeless. Our heads are full of television
But images fall apart when you enter a room.
And if not television, then words.
Poets, philosophers, intellectuals, theologians—
Can any of us truly love you?
I want to talk about kissing the small piece
Of nameless, edgeless geometry you've shown me
And how grateful I am. But should I say I'm the pond
A star fell into, or a rock?

Anyway, I can't speak about you,
Only to you, there's the whole trouble,
As if, when I tried to turn my body aside,
Some absolute force twisted it back around.
If I insist, *It's my body, my mind,*
My own mouth, I'll say what I want,
I have the right to,
You simply smile.

3. As a Jewel

Lovers think they're looking for each other
But there's only one search.

—Rumi

As a jewel compels
The gaze to caresses,
As the interrogator
Repeatedly slaps the prisoner,
As in a passing ambulance
An old man's head, rocking on its cotton pillow,
Permits itself to be glimpsed
For one instant, then vanishes
Inside its white refrigerator box
Around a corner, and that is the end of it—
Useless to shout *Come back, tell me your secret!*
So you seduce,
Hurt, and elude me,
You with your widening center
Of honey and air.

4. What You've Given Me

What's worse than having no word from you?
—Rumi

For my birthday, you came over laughing,
Set down a box with a present in it
And went away laughing.

I know what you've given me
Is inside. But sometimes I'm frightened
I'll spend my entire life

Like this, pulling off tissue
Wrappings, and never
Come to the present.

5. I'm Tired of Your Lecturing . . .

You say we need to be happy because
The material world is a door
That never closes, a gem
Of astonishing richness,
A love incapable of weakening,
Plant-life that simply grows and grows.
It's a business that won't lay off its employees,
And a terrific circus.

See? See? Of course I know all this.
Who doesn't know it?
Even my viruses want to celebrate
Both Passover and Easter
And attend the opera.
Even my white blood corpuscles intend
To vote in the next presidential election.
I love the kitchen of the world, I swear.
So please explain to me
Why I am crying now,
Why I am sick of it,
That's what's unclear.

6. *What You Want*

A half a dozen times in my existence
You have permitted me to gilmpse
Some portion of you—

The morning I lay in the bathtub
Very pregnant, and my body was
Mount Moriah, before the people
Or the goat, or the god.
The afternoon my infant son
Kicking his chubby legs
While I diapered him was also the divine
Baby, hurtling
Coldly toward me from the other world
Where everything is lightning.

The night my father
Let me know he wasn't gone
Just because he was dead, a couple of times
When a man set down his sword to let me in
To the orchard and vineyard, and the night
I was driving happy, and saw a woman
In a white gown, dancing
Where my windshield was.

No words, only supreme
Joy at being visited.

Friend, I could say
I've been alive a half a dozen moments
                    but that's not true
                    I've been alive my entire time
                        on this earth
                    I've been alive

—That's what you want me to say, isn't it.

7. What's Your Name

When I call you the One
You glance over your shoulder,
Half sneering
Like a big celebrity,
And I know you're bored.

When I call you the Many
You are suddenly here kissing me
From my feet to my mouth,
Or you're telling me funny stories
Drying my tears.

They say I should try calling you Nothing—
But I don't know
If I'm ready for that yet.

To Love Is

You do not need to accomplish the work; nor are you free to desist from it.   —The Ethics of the Fathers

i

To love is
To desire the liberty
Of the one loved

The lover thinking *Take me*
With you wherever you go
Of your own free will

Wanting to join
The dancing, the drunkenness, the kissing
On the roof, under the moon

But not to force it, not
To beg for it,
Not to be afraid it is a lie.

ii

Why all this crying?
The separated lovers
Believe they need each other

And the rejected one
Would like to hurl the rafters
Of buildings down

Or tear the mask away from a certain face
Because of its look of contempt,
While all the time

There is only the one need.

iii

And if I have desired
Since my first childish moments of sentience
When I recognized that I ardently loved the world

The balanced radiance of its good and evil
And wanted to help unlock it to become
More and more itself—

More and more alive—
What then? As I grow older
I love it less, the evil seems denser,

More strangely skewed,
My world uglier and myself weaker.
Still I keep my original loyalty,

My memory—a child on a busy
Sidewalk looking around and thinking
Beautiful dirty city, beautiful planet

I have my task,
What matter if I can
Never accomplish it.

Words for a Wedding

Free and rejoicing, walk into this prison,
The two of you,
And look around yourselves.

The important thing here isn't the rabbi
Or the feast, or even your friends and parents,
Or the musicians.

A door is clanging loudly, and finally
Here you are, noticing the stains,
Scrawls, chips in the walls, stink,

The will of those before you to escape.
Now feel in your pocket for the scrap
Of mirror the guards forgot.

Bring it forth, shyly—
You will have to share it.
And breathe easy. Finally you are here.

To One in Mourning

Because of your sorrow,
Your lost brother,
You are thinking the world is meaningless.

Now it is time for you
To swallow this wine.
Ask yourself, am I fully drunken yet?

Move

Whether it's a turtle who drags herself
Slowly to the sandlot where she digs
The sandy nest she was born to dig

And lay leathery eggs in, or whether it's salmon
Rocketing upstream
Toward pools that call: *Bring your eggs here*

And nowhere else in the world, whether it is turtle-green
Ugliness and awkwardness, or the seething
Grace and gild of silky salmon, we

Are envious, our wishes speak out right here
Thirsty for a destiny like theirs,
An absolute right choice

To end all choices. Is it memory,
We ask, is it a smell
They remember

Or just what is it, some kind of blueprint
That makes them move, hot grain by grain,
Cold cascade above icy cascade,

Slipping through
Water's fingers
A hundred miles

Inland from the easy shiny sea—
And we also, in the company
Of our tribe

Or perhaps alone, like the turtle
On her wrinkled feet with the tapping nails,
We also are going to travel, we say let's be

Oblivious to all, save
That we travel, and we say
When we reach the place we'll know

We are in the right spot, somehow, like a breath
Entering a singer's chest, that shapes itself
For the song that is to follow.

Notes

"Meditation in Seven Days": The primary sources for this poem's assumption that we may find in the text of the Bible and throughout Jewish tradition faint traces of a Canaanite goddess or goddesses whose worship was forbidden with the advent of monotheism, are Raphael Patai, *The Hebrew Goddess,* and Merlin Stone, *When God Was a Woman.* In the cabbala and other mystical writings of the late medieval and modern periods, the *Shekhina* (Heb. "dwelling, presence") is often treated as a female emanation of God's essence or as a consort of God who can only be reunited with him through Israel's fulfillment of all the divine commandments. "Torah" is often personified as a female in rabbinical writings, as is "Hokhmah," wisdom. The greeting of the Sabbath as a Bride is among the most widespread of Jewish customs. The feminist theologian Judith Plaskow argues that a genuinely nonidolatrous monotheism must ultimately incorporate images of the Goddess: "For the God who does not include her is an idol made in man's image" (*On Being a Jewish Feminist,* ed. Susannah Heschel, p. 230).

"Homage to Rumi": These and other poems in this section are in emulation of the poems of Rumi (1207–1273), the great Persian poet in whose love poems longing and absence alternate with erotic ecstasy, and the beloved friend addressed as "you" may be God, a human lover, an inner spiritual presence, or some combination of these. According to two of his translators, "Rumi is speaking of a fluctuating exchange between beings, and between beings and Being" (*Open Secret: Versions of Rumi,* trans. John Moyne and Coleman Barks, p. xi).

About the Author

Alicia Suskin Ostriker is the author of six volumes of poetry, most recently *The Imaginary Lover* (University of Pittsburgh Press), which won the 1986 William Carlos Williams Prize from the Poetry Society of America. As a critic she is the author of *Vision and Verse in William Blake* and editor of Blake's *Complete Poems*. Her writing on women poets include the essays published in *Writing Like a Woman* and *Stealing the Language: The Emergence of Women's Poetry in America*. She has received grants from the National Endowment for the Arts, the Rockefeller Foundation, and the Guggenheim Foundation. She lives in Princeton, New Jersey, and is a Professor of English at Rutgers University.

PITT POETRY SERIES

Ed Ochester, General Editor